OHIO COUNTY PUBLIC LIBRARY
WHE
26003

W9-BPP-471

A
VIKING
SETTLER

Giovanni Caselli

J
948.901
Case

AUG 1 0 1987

043100

PETER BEDRICK BOOKS
New York

Contents

Introduction — 5

On the Look-out — 6

The Market at Hedeby — 8

The Homecoming — 10

Travellers' Tales — 12

The Emperor's City — 14

Blood Feud — 16

The Meeting of the Thing — 18

A Message from England — 20

Sea Crossing — 22

Viking York — 24

The King's Hall — 26

Picture Glossary — 28

Finding Out More — 30

Introduction

This book tells the story of a young boy called Egil, who lived in the Viking town of Hedeby in Denmark in around AD 950.

It describes the adventures of his father, a brave and wealthy merchant, who makes an exciting journey across wild territory to the Swedish Viking trading post at Kiev, in modern Russia. There his father learns about the fabulous city of Constantinople, near the shores of the Black Sea. The Viking traders tell him that in Constantinople he will be able to buy precious goods from as far away as China. He decides to visit the city and, after several adventures, returns home to his family in Denmark with a new ship laden with treasures.

While Egil's father is away from home, his capable wife and family manage his farm for him. Most Vikings were farmers and traders, like Egil's father, not fierce and brutal warriors. They lived in comfortable wooden houses, grew a wide variety of crops, and raised animals.

The Vikings were also excellent sailors and boat-builders. Some Viking explorers made long journeys to look for new lands to the north and west of their homeland. A few of them even reached the east coast of America. Many more Vikings left Scandinavia to settle in the north and east of England. Some historians think that this was because there was a shortage of good farming land in Denmark. Certainly, the Vikings settled down very successfully in their new homeland. They farmed the land and also built important trading centers such as York, where Egil's family decide to go and live at the end of this story.

This book tells the story of some exciting events in the life of a young Viking boy. At the end of the book, you can see some detailed pictures of the tools and equipment Egil and his family might have used in their daily lives.

On the Look-out

Whenever Egil came into the town of
Hedeby, he begged the gatekeeper to let him
climb up to the look-out platform above the gate.
From there, he could watch the ships sailing up the
fjord from the Baltic Sea. Egil lived on a farm not far
outside the town, so the gatekeeper knew him well.

'You may go up there, Egil Erikson,' he said. 'A
fine Swedish boat has just come in!'

From the look-out platform you could see the whole
town and the great earth bank that ran round it. Egil
remembered the bank being built by order of King
Harald Bluetooth. Now people could sleep in peace,
without fear of an attack from Germans and Slavs
who came on raids across the Danish border. Far
away, looking westwards, you could see the
merchants' ox-carts setting out on their overland trek
to the great North Sea.

6

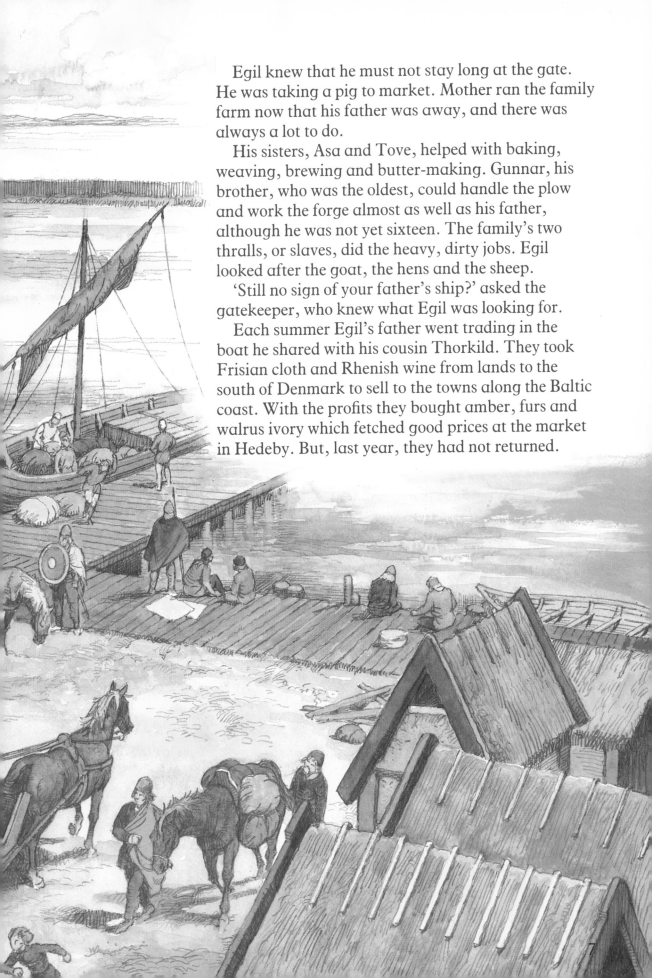

Egil knew that he must not stay long at the gate. He was taking a pig to market. Mother ran the family farm now that his father was away, and there was always a lot to do.

His sisters, Asa and Tove, helped with baking, weaving, brewing and butter-making. Gunnar, his brother, who was the oldest, could handle the plow and work the forge almost as well as his father, although he was not yet sixteen. The family's two thralls, or slaves, did the heavy, dirty jobs. Egil looked after the goat, the hens and the sheep.

'Still no sign of your father's ship?' asked the gatekeeper, who knew what Egil was looking for.

Each summer Egil's father went trading in the boat he shared with his cousin Thorkild. They took Frisian cloth and Rhenish wine from lands to the south of Denmark to sell to the towns along the Baltic coast. With the profits they bought amber, furs and walrus ivory which fetched good prices at the market in Hedeby. But, last year, they had not returned.

7

The Market at Hedeby

When he had climbed down from the look-out post, Egil continued on his way towards the center of Hedeby. First he walked past the site where the visiting merchants always camped. Then he came to the first houses. A girl drawing water from the well in her yard greeted him.

'Is all well at Gunnar's farm?' she asked.

She calls it Gunnar's farm because people believe that my father is dead, thought Egil. But I don't believe that! Surely my father is away on a great expedition, like Grandfather before him. I have heard tell of how he went raiding in England many years ago. One day my father will return with fine goods and lots of exciting stories.

As he neared the market, Egil had to push through the crowded streets. Country people had brought buckets of milk, casks of butter, and animals to sell.

Many traders had come from lands far beyond the Danish border, for Hedeby had a great market, the biggest in Denmark. Egil watched merchants leading their horses laden with cloth, traders selling pottery, glassware and fine Rhenish swords, and Norwegians unpacking cooking pots and lamps. Two Arabs were bargaining with a Viking slave-dealer. As Egil listened, the price was agreed and the dealer unfolded his scales to weigh the Arabs' silver. Just then Egil's pig, nosing for rubbish, gave a great tug at its leash. Egil's feet skidded on the wet roadway and off went the pig, rushing towards the harbor.

Egil followed it, shouting. He had no idea that pigs could run so fast! He saw it dash past some women who were washing clothes on the quay, then it disappeared from sight.

He saw the Swedish boat as he raced round the corner. The owner, to judge from the number of his silver arm-rings, was a very rich man. Slowly, the man turned round to face him. It was his father, home at last!

9

The Homecoming

The pig was nowhere to be found, but that didn't matter. Egil greeted his father joyfully. He had so many questions to ask! Father explained that Cousin Thorkild was bringing their old boat home. They had bought the new Swedish boat because they had so many treasures to carry home. He ordered his men to finish unloading the boat, while he and Egil set off for the farm.

The farm, though not as big as a nobleman's or earl's, was really quite large. Its meadows provided enough hay to keep twenty cattle through the winter. The farmhouse, with its long cowshed attached, stood in the middle of a big yard. Egil ran to open the gate. The thrall who was cleaning out the shed yelled in amazement as the cart trundled in. Gunnar was in the forge mending tools; the second thrall was lighting the fire in the bakehouse. They both ran out at the noise.

Everyone followed father into the house. Mother, all floury from grinding the rye, leaped to her feet to meet him. Tove left her weaving.

'Call Asa,' said Mother. 'She has taken the cows to the far pasture.'

Egil ran through the bean field and along the edge of the oats and the barley, calling to his sister. She could hardly believe the news and rushed back to the house in great excitement.

Father spread out gifts for everyone. There were silver drinking cups and sweet-smelling spices for the whole family to enjoy. He gave lengths of silk cloth and silver neckbands to Mother and the girls. For Gunnar, there was a sword, and to Egil he gave a silver charm and a beautiful knife. They all gasped with pleasure and thanked Father. How wonderful it was to have him home again!

'We will sacrifice an ox,' said Mother, 'and set it outside the door to thank the god Thor for Father's safe return.'

Travellers' Tales

That night they had a happy dinner together. Mother told Father all the news about the farm; how six new calves had been born safely in the spring and that the harvest promised to be a good one.

After dinner, they sat round Father and begged him to tell them his story.

'Last year we met a company of Swedish merchants who took us to a trading town they have built far along the Baltic, in the land of the Finns and Slavs. The people of that land are afraid of the Swedes and they have cause to be. The winters there are bitterly cold, and the Swedes raid the villages and live well. In the spring they travel south to Kiev, a town far inland. The Swedes told us that merchants travel to Kiev from many lands. You can sell fur and slaves there for a much higher price than at Hedeby, and you can buy goods that will make your fortune at home. We decided to join them in their winter raids and see if we could take enough slaves to make the trip south worthwhile. Thor gave us luck and by spring we had plenty of slaves, fur, honey and wax. We prepared for the long journey to Kiev.

'When the snows melted we took a fleet of river boats and followed the Swedes along a wide river. We sailed upstream between huge forests where robbers lie in wait. At night we camped on the banks, but we always slept with our hands on our swords. We stopped at many of the riverside towns, but our Swedish companions said that Kiev was still many weeks ahead. The river grew narrower. We rowed until it was a trickle no wider than our boats. Then we made the slaves drag the boats overland and carry them over the roughest ground, until we reached a stream that flowed south. This brought us, at last, to the great walled town of Kiev.

'Many of the Swedes have made their homes there, and rule the Slavs. They have taken Slav wives and dress and speak live Slavs. We sold our goods and slaves without difficulty and bought silks from merchants who came from China at the eastern edge of the world, from Samarkand and from Baghdad.'

The Emperor's City

Father continued the story of his adventures.

'In summer the Swedish traders travel south from Kiev to the city of the Christian emperor of the east. It lies in the land of the Greeks, who call it Constantinople. We decided to go too, to sell the rest of our slaves and to see what we could buy. The Swedes travel in a great fleet for safety. The river passes through plains where savage tribes live. The river, too, is treacherous. It rushes between narrow gorges in many rapids and cataracts. Sometimes we had to carry the boats along the edge of the rapids. The most terrible rapid is called "The Ever-Fierce". We had to walk six miles overland to pass it! Wild tribes were lying in wait for us, and attacked us with stones and arrows. We needed all our numbers to fight them off and many good men were killed.

'Beyond the rapids there is an island with a sacred oak tree. We made sacrifices of bread and meat there to give thanks for our safe passage.

'At last the river carried us to a sea without a tide, which the local people call the Black Sea. In those lands the Sun's horse rides so close to the Earth that the light from his mane is dazzling. We followed the coast till we came to Constantinople – the emperor's city. Its palaces are made of stone and are decorated with gold. Its people know strange arts. They can lift up rivers on bridges of stone and have built a mighty temple with a round roof of stone which hangs in the air without pillars.

'The Greeks like Vikings to do their fighting for them. Many Swedes serve in their army and in the emperor's bodyguard. I met one who showed me round the emperor's palace, which is full of wonders. Then we journeyed home with profits beyond our wildest dreams.'

Blood Feud

Egil was delighted with his new knife. No Viking freeman ever went unarmed, for he never knew when he might need to fight. News which arrived at the farm the next day showed how close danger could be.

While Cousin Thorkild's family had been celebrating his homecoming, their house had been surrounded by Tostig and his men. They were members of a neighboring family who had a long-standing feud with Thorkild's kinsmen. Tostig had threatened to set fire to the house if Thorkild did not come out. To save his family, Thorkild had rushed out to face his attackers. He had wounded many before being overpowered and killed.

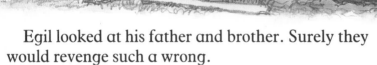

Egil looked at his father and brother. Surely they would revenge such a wrong.

'Tostig shall suffer for this!' said Father. 'But first we will honor Thorkild. He died with his sword in his hand! He must have all he needs in the land beyond the grave. He shall take our new ship with him, well stocked for the journey.'

In the days that followed, many preparations were made for Thorkild's funeral. Egil went to help drag the new boat overland to the burial place.

On the day of the funeral, Thorkild's body was placed in a wooden chamber on the boat's deck. His sword, shield and spear were set beside him. His horse and hunting dogs were killed and laid in the ship.

They would live again with their master in his new life beyond the grave. He was given gold and silver arm-bands, food for the journey, cups and cooking pots. Then the ship was covered in a mound of earth. Thorkild's widow placed a carved stone, which recorded Thorkild's name and his heroic death, beside the mound. Then the family went sadly home.

The Meeting of the Thing

At the funeral feast Father announced his decision. He would summon Tostig to appear at the meeting of the Thing to answer for Thorkild's killing. He would ask the judges to impose a heavy punishment. Family honor would be satisfied and the feud would be settled.

The Thing was an assembly of all the freemen of the district. It was held several times a year to decide important matters of trade and government. It made new laws and judged disputes. Every man who owned property could vote when decisions were made.

On the first day of the Thing, Father and Gunnar, in their finest clothes, set off early for the Thingstead, the place where the meetings were always held. They had to make sure that all their kinsmen were present to swear that what they said was true. Egil followed with a cart loaded with camping equipment. The Thing lasted several days, so most people brought tents and cooking utensils, and often some goods to sell. Women did not take part, so it was Egil's job to set up the tent and see that meals were ready. He must also listen and learn, for soon he would be old enough to vote.

The Thingstead was on Earl Svein's land. The local earls sat on a slope with the judges they had chosen to decide the case. First the lawspeaker recited the law, for Viking laws were learnt by heart, not written down. Then Egil's father told of the feud between his kinsmen and some of Tostig's family, in which Cousin Thorkild had played no part at all. Next Tostig spoke. It was right, he said, to avenge a great wrong by slaying the senior member of a family. True, said the judges, but the manner of the killing was cowardly and vile. For that Tostig must be outlawed.

'What will happen to him?' asked Egil.

'He will leave the country,' said Gunnar, 'because if we find him here we may lawfully kill him.'

A Message from England

Egil rather hoped that Gunnar would seek out Tostig to avenge Thorkild's death, because he wanted to join in the attack. But soon new plans made everyone forget the hunt for Tostig. A messenger brought news from England, where Cousin Halfdan had settled. He had grown rich as a merchant in the Viking city of York. His wife was now begging Egil's father to come and live in England, since Halfdan was on the point of death. There was no one else to continue Halfdan's business or to protect her daughter, for they had no kinsmen there.

The matter was soon settled.

'Gunnar will stay in Denmark,' said Erik. 'He will marry Cousin Thorkild's daughter, and take over Thorkild's estate. Then he will have almost as much land as Earl Svein. Egil and the women will sail with me for York, and we shall take over Halfdan's business.'

Egil wondered if Gunnar minded marrying his cousin, who was neither good-tempered nor beautiful. But Gunnar would do as his father wished, and so would she.

Gunnar was to keep the old trading boat, and so a new ship would be needed for the voyage. Egil and his father went to the boatbuilders' yard. All kinds of craft were being made; many small rowing boats, a flat-bottomed ferry boat and, almost completed, a splendid longship large enough to carry fifty armed raiders. Egil wished he could sail in a warship! Instead, he turned to look at the craftsmen at work on his family's boat. Some men were splitting oak logs into planks, while others were fastening the curved prow and stern pieces to the keel to make the backbone of the ship. They would build the hull out of rows of overlapping planks. Egil sniffed at a vat of tarred animal hair.

'That will go·between the planks to keep the water out,' said one of the men. 'Then we'll make the inner framework, the ribs and the cross-beams. Below the waterline, we'll lash it to the hull with tree-roots. Nailing it all together would make the ship too rigid. She must be supple to ride the waves!'

Sea Crossing

Egil knew how to handle a small boat, and had often been fishing along the coast. But he had never been so far from land before. They had been at sea now for three days. Yesterday they had run into a great storm. They had had to lift the loose planks on the lower deck and bail out the water trapped below in wooden scoops. Despite his cloak of skins, Egil had been drenched. At night, in his wet clothes, he had been bitterly cold. With all the household gear and food, there was only room to put up one tent. His parents slept in that, though Father spent most of the night guiding the oar-shaped rudder that steered the boat. His sisters shared one skin sleeping bag and the thralls shared another, but Egil shivered on his own. Today the sun shone, but the waves were as high as ever.

A terrible fear seized Egil. He knew that the World Serpent wrapped itself round the edge of the world. Suppose they had sailed too far, and the sea was being lashed by its tail? Egil dared not ask his father what he thought, for a Viking must not show fear. Instead he said, 'Is England the last land before the edge of the world?'

'No,' said Father, 'the Norwegians have sailed far round it to the North, to a land beyond called Ireland. They have taken land there and built towns. Northwest again, they have found an empty land they call Iceland. Whenever Vikings sail west they find new lands. Many more may lie ahead.'

'But how do we know we are sailing the right way?' asked Egil.

'By the position of the Pole Star and the Sun,' said Father. He showed Egil how the shadow of a wooden pin on a special instrument told him which way to steer. 'And look,' he said, 'that flight of birds shows that land is near. It won't be long before we reach England.'

Viking York

Egil felt at home in York. The buildings reminded him of Denmark. This was not surprising, for much of the town had been built by Vikings. They had taken this land, Northumbria, from the Anglo-Saxons, and now a Viking king, Erik Bloodaxe, ruled in the north and east of England. The Anglo-Saxons had taken it from the Britons long ago, and even before that a conquering race from faraway Italy had built a great stone city at York. Part of the Roman walls remained for Egil to see.

Egil was glad to be sent out of the house to buy oysters. He enjoyed looking around the town and he decided to take the longest route back home. He turned along Cupmakers' Street to dawdle outside the workshops. He watched a woodworker turning bowls of ash and yew, and the jewellers making amber pendants and necklaces of jet. The bone-carver was setting out his combs, pins and needles, and his assistant was dyeing bone buckles. Next door was a leather shop, but the hides were smelly and Egil did not linger. He caught sight of a row of decorated axe-blades on a metal-worker's stall and stopped for a closer look.

The shop's owner was striking coins. He placed a disk of silver between two dies and with one hammer-blow he punched a design on both sides. Thor's hammer and the name Peter were imprinted on the coin.

'Who is Peter?' Egil asked.

The coiner was English but Egil could understand his answer well enough.

'Peter is the patron saint of York and the chief servant of Christ.'

'In Denmark we laugh at Christians,' said Egil. 'Their church bells annoy the gods.'

'We are all Christians here and no one laughs at us!' said the coiner's son, a big boy, older than Egil. 'Of course it is wise to worship the old gods as well. Even the king, Erik Bloodaxe, has become a Christian. He is a Viking and one of the greatest warlords of Odin, god of war.'

The King's Hall

'My father works for the Master of the King's Mint. The Master controls the making of coins,' said the coiner's son, whose name was Alfric. 'He has placed me in the King's service. There is to be a big feast today, and I have to pour wine and beer for the feasters. Would you like to come to the King's Hall with me? There will be lots to see.'

Egil agreed gladly. The King's Hall was larger than any house he had ever been in. A great fire blazed in the center, filling the Hall with light. Long tables on trestles had been set up for the feasting. Silver drinking cups were waiting to be filled. Before the feast began, King Erik Bloodaxe called for a great wooden chest to be brought to him. From it he took neck-rings and arm-rings of silver and gold, and gave them to his followers to thank them for their part in his recent victory over King Eadred.

As Alfric explained to Egil, 'Eadred of the West Saxons would like to think of himself as King of all England, but we Northumbrians want a King of our own! Erik Bloodaxe and his warriors gave Eadred a good hiding. I don't think he'll be back for a while!'

Suddenly the shouting and laughter died away. The king's Skald had begun to sing about the battle. He was a good poet, and one of the king's most important servants. He went with him into battle and watched everything that happened. Later, he composed wonderful songs to be sung on great occasions like this. People would remember his words for years to come. In this way, great men and their deeds would never be forgotten.

The Skald raised his voice and sang of the valor of Erik Bloodaxe and his men. 'Their swords shone with bright blood . . . Odin, god of war, will reward them in Valhalla when they enter the Hall of the Slain.'

Egil listened, spellbound. In this, his new homeland, he meant to become a great warrior like Erik Bloodaxe and these men, and to fight with the brave Northumbrians against King Eadred of Wessex. He could hardly wait!

Picture Glossary

Vikings living in different parts of Scandinavia formed three distinct groups: the Danes, the Swedes and the Norwegians. Each group set off in a different direction for its voyages of plunder, trade or exploration, as the map below shows.

Our best sources of information about the everyday lives of the Vikings are the many archaeological remains that survive from the Viking period. Coins, weapons, jewelry, cooking pots, and remains of ships all help archaeologists to build up a picture of life in Viking times.

Vikings made many beautiful objects out of metal, as well as dangerous weapons of war. They forged locally-produced iron to make heavy farm equipment, and traded for jewels and precious metals with merchants from distant lands, or seized them as plunder.

They also loved jewelry and display, and many examples of Viking workmanship can still be seen in museums today.

The drawings on these two pages are all based on real-life objects discovered by archaeologists at Viking sites.

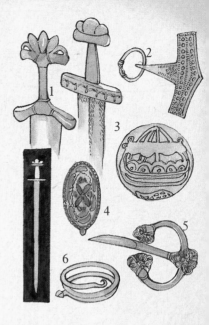

Metalwork
1 Sword handles
2 Silver pendant
3 Silver coin
4 Bronze brooch
5 Cloak fastener
6 Silver bracelet

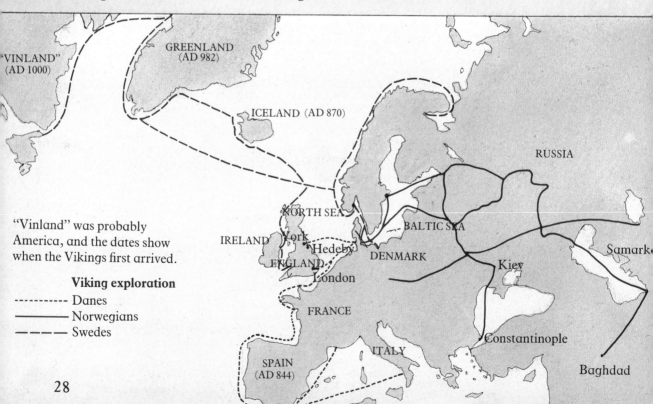

"Vinland" was probably America, and the dates show when the Vikings first arrived.

Viking exploration
- - - - - - - Danes
————— Norwegians
– – – – Swedes

"VINLAND" (AD 1000)

GREENLAND (AD 982)

ICELAND (AD 870)

RUSSIA

NORTH SEA

BALTIC SEA

IRELAND

York

Hedeby

DENMARK

Kiev

ENGLAND

London

Samark

FRANCE

Constantinople

ITALY

SPAIN (AD 844)

Baghdad

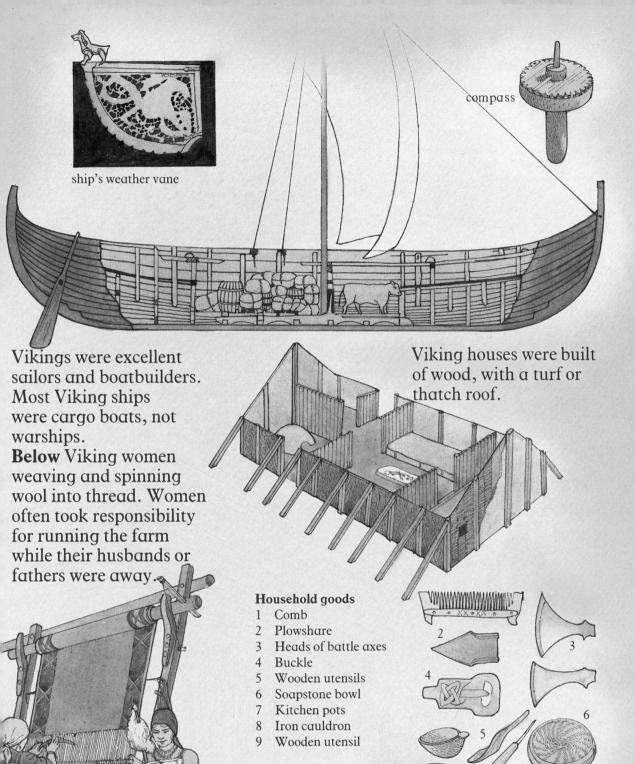

ship's weather vane

compass

Vikings were excellent sailors and boatbuilders. Most Viking ships were cargo boats, not warships.
Below Viking women weaving and spinning wool into thread. Women often took responsibility for running the farm while their husbands or fathers were away.

Viking houses were built of wood, with a turf or thatch roof.

Household goods
1 Comb
2 Plowshare
3 Heads of battle axes
4 Buckle
5 Wooden utensils
6 Soapstone bowl
7 Kitchen pots
8 Iron cauldron
9 Wooden utensil

Runes, the Viking alphabet, were cut into wood.

PRINTED IN BELGIUM BY

INTERNATIONAL BOOK PRODUCTION

Finding Out More

Books to Read

The following books all contain information about the Vikings:

I. Atkinson **The Viking Ships** Cambridge University
    Press 1978
G. Caselli **The Roman Empire and the Dark Ages**
    Peter Bedrick Books 1985
M. Gibson **The Vikings** Macdonald Educational 1976
R. Hall **The Viking Dig** The Bodley Head 1984
R. Waites **Children's York** Redcliffe 1984
P. Wenham **Saxon and Viking Britain**
    Hutchinson 1979